C# for Beginners

A Complete C# Programming Guide to Getting You Started Right Away!
(2022 Crash Course for All)

Cary Gregory

Table of Contents

Thank you for buying C# for Beginners and congratulations for doing so. The next chapters will cover all you need to know to get started with the C# programming language.

Many various pieces come with this language, and being able to set it up properly and ensuring that you will be able to produce some strong programs, as a result, will be a vital part of the process. To begin our journey, we'll take a deeper look at the C# programming language. We'll go over the advantages of using this language, look at some of the tools we'll need to make this coding language function, and even go over some of the steps we can take to create our first piece of code in this language. This section will also be examined so that we can understand how to build up the C# environment with all of the necessary components. When we finish this kind of introduction, we'll move on to some of the various components that come with the C# language, and we'll learn how to apply them to our requirements.

We'll look at a few different options, such as how to work with C# variables, their importance, the various types of operators in this language, and even how to go through and create some of our conditional statements so that our programs can make their own decisions even if we aren't there to help them with every possible input. Following that, we'll have a look at the steps you may take to construct your objects and define your classes. Both of these subjects are vital when dealing with an OOP language like C#, and we'll spend some time looking at how to work with them alone and together, as well as some code to get it all done. We'll spend some time in this handbook developing some of the essential loops, which is another cool thing we can accomplish inside of this language. There are many different types of loops, and we'll go through a few of them, but they all help us decrease the amount of space our code takes up, save time, and contain a lot of information in a short bit of code.

After that, we'll take a look at a couple more crucial issues to wrap out this handbook. These include a look at the strings, lists, and arrays that will be used a lot in the code you'll be writing. On the surface, they may seem to be the same or extremely similar, but the more you deal with code, the better you will need to grasp them.

After that, we'll have a look at some of the greatest tips and methods that a newbie programmer may utilize to help them succeed with the C# language in general. There are several wonderful coding languages out there, but none of them will give us the greatest frameworks, the most power, and all of the incredible features that we will see while utilizing the C# language. This handbook spent time learning more about it and how we might use it to our objectives.

When you're ready to learn more about the C# programming language and want to get started straight away, this manual will come in handy. There are many books on this topic available; thank you for selecting this one! It was designed with great care to provide as much valuable information as possible. Please have pleasure in it.

Chapter 1:

What is C#?

When it comes to programming and all of the things you can do with it, one of the cool things about it is that there are quite a few different programming languages to pick from.

Each has been developed to handle a certain kind of coding need, allowing us to focus on the aspects of our projects and requirements that are most essential to us.However, C# is one of the coding languages on which we will spend considerable time in this handbook.

Most individuals who are interested in learning to code but have never done it before will find it easy to be concerned about the whole process when it comes time to learn anything new.

They understand that coding is beneficial and can help them in a variety of ways, but they are concerned that it will be too difficult.

They may utilize it to make their apps, websites, and programs, and it could even be the key to unlocking some new career doors.

However, they are concerned that learning to code will be too difficult due to all of the additional alternatives accessible while working with this method.

If you allow your fear and anxiety to get the best of you and you don't take the time to learn one of these new languages, the programming process and the procedures required to work on them will be very tough for you to manage.

However, you will discover that selecting a decent language to work with, such as the simplicity and amazing features of the C# language, will make it much simpler to manage all of your projects, whether you have previously learned how to program or this is your first time.

With this in mind, it's time to go in a little further and learn more about the C# process, what we can achieve with this language that is so much better than some of the other possibilities, and so much more.

Why should you learn C#?

The first question we must address is why we would want to learn how to use the C# programming language.

There are many alternative coding and programming languages on which we may spend our time, and many of them can give us the advantages we need.

So, why would we want to learn more about C# and how it can be used to meet our requirements as well?

As we previously said, there is a plethora of various coding and programming languages from which to choose, each of which will function differently and provide us with unique advantages.

It's often difficult to figure out which one is the best fit for us.

Some programmers may choose one based on how simple it seems, while others will learn one because it can do the jobs they are interested in.

However, no matter what your coding goal is in the first place, working with the C# language will give you several advantages, which we will go over in this part.

Even if you are a beginner, understanding some of these advantages will help us gain confidence in the coding language, and you will discover that this will enable us to create some very great programs and apps in the process.

The following are some of the advantages of using the C# programming language:

1. The C# library is far bigger than many other libraries, allowing you to do a lot more in the process. There will be many aspects of your code that will not come as easy as you would want as a novice without some practice.

The good news is that the C# library will offer you some of the assistance you need.

You may easily add the required functions to the code without much effort.

You can even use them to make adjustments to your code to guarantee that it works the way you want it to.

2. It will automatically disable the functionalities for you.

After you're working with other coding languages, you'll be responsible for eliminating the functions when they're finished on your own.

This may be time-consuming and inconvenient, particularly if you forget a few.

One of the advantages of the C# programming language is that it will take care of this for you, making the whole process much simpler.

3. The C# programming language is simple to learn for novices.

In fact, most people believe this to be the simplest of all the programming languages to learn.

While there will be a few aspects that add extra complexity to the mix, you will discover that you can identify and utilize the various components of the C# language with fairly ease for the most part.

4. The C# programming language was created with Windows in mind, but it may also be used on any other platform you choose.

This language will run on Linux, Mac, and Windows as long as you get the.NET framework as well.

However, since Windows has several extra goods and features that assist novices in learning this language, it is frequently the recommended technique to use with this language. If you are still unsure about which operating system to use, Windows is the way to go.

5. The.NET framework will be your best buddy during this process and will make coding simpler.

This will be an application that is freely accessible on Windows computers, so you will not have to go out of your way to get it.

It is, however, simple to install on other operating systems, so this should not be an issue.

6. The C# language will have a lot in common with the C++ and C languages.

If you already know how to code using this application, this will make it a lot simpler for us to learn how to perform programming and some of the fundamentals.

Even if you stick to this language and don't branch out to other languages, you'll discover that the C# language has all of the strength you need to complete your codes and programs.

Where Do I Begin?

Now that we've learned a little more about some of the advantages of the C# programming language, it's time to look at some of the procedures required to get started.

One of the first things we should verify before starting any coding is whether we have the.NET framework, which we discussed before since this is the environment in which we will be writing our own code.

If you're using Windows, you should already have a development kit on your machine.

This will be a required framework to use starting with the Windows Vista edition of the Windows operating system family, thus you should check to see whether the.NET framework is installed on your computer if you are using that operating system or newer.

You won't need to download it since your machine is unlikely to be running an outdated operating system right now.

However, if you're going through this procedure and your Windows machine doesn't have the.NET framework installed, or you're using another operating system that doesn't have this framework installed by default, it's time to get to work.

For Mac and Linux, the Mono Project will be a little simpler to use and will perform better than the.NET framework on these platforms.

You may still locate it in the Microsoft Store, and then just follow the on-screen instructions to have it downloaded to your computer.

You may also receive the necessary file from the website www.monoporject.com.

Now that we have the proper structure in place, we can begin working on some of the other things we need to accomplish with the C# language.

Assuming that you have completed all of the required downloads for the frameworks and tools that you need, or that they are already installed on your PC, it is now time to begin learning how to use the C# language. When we perform some of this on our Windows machine, you'll see that the C# language is really easy to use.

The reason for this is that the Windows operating system will automatically be compatible with our.NET framework, and when this is combined with the fact that the C# language is an easy and flexible one to learn, you will be able to pick up on some of the coding's in no time.

All of this will be available to assist you while also giving you the power you need to keep all of your codes safe.

For someone who is completely new to all of the concepts we're discussing here when it comes to coding and programming, you'll discover that this language provides us with the essential simplicity of use while yet giving us the strength to complete our scripts.

C# does not allow code pointers, which is similar to what you'll discover when working with many other programming languages, including Java. This is also not one of the languages that can handle the so-called multiple inheritances procedure.

Certain of this must be remembered since it is something that some other coding languages can handle, and you don't want to be caught off guard later.

However, instead of providing some of these alternatives, the C# language will supply you with a few others, such as type checking and memory collection.

Other vital and strong elements of the C++ language are readily apparent, which you may use as part of your programs depending on our goals.

When it comes to working in the C# language, there are a lot of parts that we can use, so let's delve into some of the real codings and discover how this works so we can see some of these parts in action.

Developing a C# Program

Now that we've covered some of the groundwork, it's time to get down to business and see how we can develop our first C# application.

This is the part you've been looking forward to.

We don't want to hear a few words on the language and then nothing further, no concrete measures to take.

But that's why we're going to spend so much time in this part laying up one of the C# routines we want to employ.

So, to get started creating this code, we'll need to open up our text editor and have the C# language set up and ready to go.

If you're doing this on a Windows device, all you have to do is open Notepad to get started.

There are other alternatives as well, so think about it before you start working on the code, and then have it installed and ready to use on your computer.

Once you've got a chance to open up your preferred editor, whether it's Notepad or anything else, enter in the following code to get some practice:

```
class FirstProgram
{
static void Main()
{
Console.WriteLine("Using C# is fun.");
}
}
```

You may now enter the command prompt by typing:

```
csc FirstProgram.cs
```

Following this command, the C# compiler will analyze the file and build an.exe file in the same directory as your code.

If you saved the original file to the desktop, for example, a new application named "FirstProgram.ee." should appear in the same location.

If there is a problem with the code you wrote, an error message will appear. By typing "FirstProgram.exe." into the command line, you can now launch this program. If everything went well, you should see the following message on the command prompt: "Using C# is enjoyable."

After you've had an opportunity to work with this software, it's time for us to take some time to study it and see how it works.

We can see from the code we worked on before that it is a straightforward procedure to deal with. Despite the seeming simplicity, we can see that several pieces and features of code have to come together to make this one function.

The following are some of the most significant areas of the code that we must concentrate on:

1. Take a look at the first line of the paragraph.This is where we should put a suitable identification as well as a keyword.The keyword will be the primary term in the code that performs a certain function and may instruct the compiler on how to proceed. We're directing the compiler to build a new class for the program using the keyword in our example. After that, the identifier will be responsible for listing the variable, class, andmethod. We're going to use one called "FirstProgram" in that example.

2. After that, we may go to the third line of the whole thing. This is where we'll put the name of the Main() function. On the PC, this will be the beginning point for our program.
When we have this, the program will be able to begin by running this method, regardless of where you put it in your code. After then, there will be two terms that may be used in this method: void and static. These will then assist us in determining which object will be encountered in the code.

3. We may now go on to the fifth line. This is the last and most important section of the code that we wrote earlier.This is the line where we may type a message that will appear on the computer screen after the program has been performed. The WriteLine() function will be used here so that the compiler understands that the statement you're adding is expected to be shown.

Braces appeared in the code along the way, in addition to some of the other subjects we discussed before.

These are also important to the code that we want to create since they are in charge of informing our computer that there are a lot of blocks of code that need to be split throughout, and they will help us keep everything neat and organized as we go.

Chapter 2:
How to Install the C# Programming Language

While we did spend some time in the last chapter looking at how to create some code in the C# language, we got a little ahead of ourselves. Now it's time to take a step back and review some of the fundamentals that we'll need to know in order to fully understand how to set up the C# language on our PCs.

We'll also look at how to use.NET Core and Visual Studio, and how they'll work together on our application to get the greatest results.

You will discover that when you combine the C# language that we are discussing here with the Visual Studio that we will present later, it will offer us all of the essential editing expertise that we need to get things to function correctly.

While we combine all of these capabilities and advantages with the excellent support provided by C# IntelliSense, which is what we will use when creating our code, and some assistance with the debugging process, we will be well on our way to writing our own code.

Along the process, you'll discover that the C# programming language, as well as some of the tools required to make it work, are already installed on a computer running the Windows operating system. This is a language that works for hand in hand with Windows, making things simpler if you already have and want to utilize that operating system.

The good news is that this language can also be used on the other two major operating systems, but it will require some additional effort to get it there, and the number of features available when using C# on Mac or Linux may be restricted. Even if your aim is to use the C# language on a Windows PC, you must first complete the essential procedures to install Visual Studio with C#.

This Microsoft Visual Studio will be one of your alternatives for an integrated development environment or IDE, and it is already available for us to utilize from Microsoft. When using C# for programming, it is often the best option. You'll also need to go through and put in a lot of effort to have all of the pieces together and ready for your program.

And you'll discover that Visual Studio can aid you with the.NET framework as well.

It will be the one-stop-shop that we need for the apps that we want to develop using this platform and language; therefore, it is worth our time to learn more about it.

It will be much simpler for us to get our apps to generate, execute, and go through the debugging process with the aid of Visual Studio.

We may concentrate on a few various sorts of apps here, such as forms-based and web-based, and they will all be available to create on your IDE when you're ready.

Visual Studio will be able to provide us with all of the features we need to complete this task.

With all of this information in mind, we should spend some time looking at the many processes that must be followed in order to download and install the Visual Studio IDE and utilize it for our purposes.

When we've finished installing the IDE, we'll be able to use it to do all of our programming tasks.

The following are the easy methods we may utilize to install the IDE:

1. You must first go to the Visual Studio website and download all of the necessary files and resources.
   https://www.visualstudio.com/downloads/ is one of the websites you may work with.

   a. You have the option of choosing between the Community and Professional Editions. The first will be free, while the second will be a little more expensive. We'll look at how to install the professional version since it contains more of the features you're searching for.

2. After selecting your version, double-click the.exe file you just downloaded.

3. Make sure you click to continue when you come to the next screen.

4. At this point, we'll start with some of the downloading operations that Visual Studio requires.
   This will include all of the basic files that you will need.
   Keep in mind that the download speed will vary depending on your internet connection and how quickly it can manage the workload.

5. After that, we'll be presented with a new screen. On the version of the Visual Studio IDE that you want to use, click install.

6. At this point, we'll go on to the next screen, where we'll discover a plethora of alternatives to pick from.

Our aim is to select.NET desktop development and then go through the installation procedure to have it installed on our desktop PC before we start coding.

7. The next step is for Visual Studio to spend some time obtaining the files you need depending on the various choices you made before.

   You may just click on the portions we recommended, or you can go through and make some changes if you like.

8. Once we've finished getting that download underway, the computer will ask you to restart it.

   This must be done in order to get everything in order, so accept to work on it and restart the computer.

9. Once the reboot is complete, which might take a few minutes, open the computer and search for the Visual Studio IDE that we just worked on.

   You can then utilize this IDE by opening it up as follows:

   An a. Once we've opened it up, we should be able to choose the theme we wish to utilize.

   This isn't going to be a big deal, and you may use whatever one you like for your code. An a. Once you've decided, click Continue using Visual Studio to get started.

10. Once we've arrived in the Visual Studio IDE, we'll need to move around a little to locate the File Menu.

    After that, you must click on the menu, then seek the section that says "build a new C# program" and click on it.

11. You may now complete the rest of the procedure by following all of the essential stages. When you've completed all of the stages, you'll be able to effortlessly type down the various codes you wish to employ with the C# language.

You'll find that there are several reasons why you should use this IDE instead of others.

Yes, a short search will reveal that there are other solutions available, but none of them will give us the same level of functionality.

For example, this Visual Studio IDE will make it easy for us to construct custom apps in any of the.NET framework's supported languages.

This gives you a little more flexibility in your demands.

It's also an IDE that will enable us to construct all of the different sorts of apps we need.

The IDE from Visual Studio is an excellent alternative to assist in troubleshooting some of your scripts if you're just getting started with coding and learning the ropes a little bit.

There will always be moments when your code will run into problems, and knowing able to debug it will guarantee that it operates the way you want it to.

When we utilize the Visual Studio IDE, we may test out some of the apps we're working on as we're trying to build them up.

This will save us a lot of time and enable us to learn on the job so that we can grow better at some of the codings we want to perform.

All of the amazing extensions that come with it will make learning how to work with this coding language a lot more enjoyable overall.

While there are many alternatives for learning C#, you will discover that the IDE that comes with Visual Studio is one of the finest, and if you follow the procedures in this chapter, you will have it all downloaded and set up so that you can start working on some of the coding's you want.

Chapter 3:

The Variables and How to Work With Them

When it comes to our variables, the first thing we need to look at is all of the various forms of data that can be discovered using the C# language. When working with this, you may break it into two primary pieces, each of which is distinct yet complementary.

These will be divided into two categories: "value type" and "reference type."

When we look at the value kinds in more detail, keep in mind that the data must be supplied via the method you want to utilize.

However, if you're dealing with a reference type of these, you'll need to be sure to include information about our function since the value will be placed somewhere else in the code.

We may use the following categories of information:

Along with Double Long Float Unit Int Ushort Sbyte Short Byte Bool—when using this type, the maximum number of values you can store is two.

Because the values are false and true, it's appropriate for conditional statements and logical expressions.

Decimal Char—this is a data type that can only hold one single character. When writing the char value, you must surround it with single quotes, such as 't', 'b', and so on.

Variables in C#

You'll discover that no matter how much code you create, you'll eventually need to go through and run it.

When it's time to run the code, the computer software will save the information until it's time to run it again.

The variables are the best method for us to store this information.

To make things as simple as possible, a variable will set aside a space in our computers' memory to retain the data you're trying to produce.

Because of these characteristics, the variables will always have at least one value, and occasionally many values at the same time.

This value will then be saved to the memory location where we previously stored the variable.

We can use the syntax to assist you to construct a new variable while working with this language:

a variable name> a data type> a variable name> a variable name> a variable_

When you enter the following code into your compiler, you are creating a variable that will save a section of memory for you to store a value in.

The programmer will then be able to use the identification assigned to this variable to access it.

If you had written the formula above as char x, for example, you might locate the variable by looking up x.

When it comes to declaring variables, C# is special in that it will assist us in initializing some of the variables we wish to utilize.

This word refers to the process of assigning a value to a variable after it has been created.

All you have to do is utilize one of the assignment operators, and the operator we require here is the equal sign. When you're finished, you may write down the value you wish to put there.

Another option is to define many variables at once in the same line, as long as we are dealing with the same kind of data.

All we have to do now is make sure that each of the items we add to that statement has a comma between them to help them stand out. However, while we're here, we should double-check that the variables have been defined before attempting to access and utilize them in our code.

The C# language will also need us to implement a new rule, which we will refer to as a definite assignment. This implies that you'll have to spend some time programming to set up the local variables you wish to utilize before you can use them in some of the code you write.

Then, utilizing the procedure we just discussed in the process, you can go through and assign the initial value of our local variable when declaring it.

One thing to keep in mind as we go through this phase and utilize this language is that the variables we'll use will be named using this manner as well since the values that the variables should contain will change each time you execute and run the program.

Your values will change, but what they become will mostly rely on what you want them to be for the code to operate.

How to Make a Unique Identifier

One of the good things about Microsoft is that it will present you with a range of options for getting C# to operate properly.

And one of these suggestions is that C# programmers should use the Camel notation in their work and with the variables they create.

Then, while working with the techniques we've discussed, you'll need to deal using a little different way known as "the Pascal notation."

This may seem confusing to a newbie, so let's have a look at them.

When using the Camel notation, ensure sure the variable name's initial letter is lower case.

If you want your new identifier or variable to be a compound word, the initial letter of the second word must be uppercase.

This helps to keep them distinct and makes it simpler to read them.

The following is an example of some of the codes that may be written in camel case:

Payment complete
Payment mathematics firstclass

Things will be handled a little differently in Pascal's notation.

You must begin the first word with an uppercase letter in this notation style.

All of the other words in the series should have their initial letter in uppercase as well. The following are some instances of Pascal notation:

WriteLine () ReadLine()

Start () Main ()

You'll be able to use digits and underscores as well as letters when naming these identifiers.

These IDs, however, will not be allowed to begin with a number.

You could write out seven books, but you couldn't write out seven books.

When working on this, it's important to realize that the notations aren't always necessary, and you may make some adjustments to utilize them to help us identify the identifiers if you like.

However, since the Pascal and Camel notations will be viewed as the right method to do things in code, it is advisable to utilize them so that other programmers understand what you're talking about.

As we can see, even for a newbie, working with the C# language is not that difficult.

There will be a lot of pieces that come together that we'll need to remember as we go along, and it may be difficult to keep track of everything with all of the regulations.

But as we go through our coding, we'll discover why these components are in there, and why they're critical to some of the work we want to perform with our scripts.

Chapter 4

Handling C# Operators

It's difficult to have a proper conversation about the C# language if we don't explain the operators and how they're meant to operate in some of our programs.

These are a pretty basic choice that we can manage, but they will be crucial in ensuring that our scripts run properly. In fact, in the previous chapter on variables, we spent some time discussing one of the operators, the assignment operators.

These operators will appear in our code all over the place, so it's time to understand what they are, what they signify, and how to utilize them.

There are a few distinct sorts of operators that we may use in our code, and each one will play a different function in the process.

They'll all have their task to do no matter how you use them in the scripts you create.

We'll be able to implement some of the functionality we want after we've included the appropriate operators.

These operators will be simpler to use than you may expect, but the functionality and power that they provide will be incredible.

The nice thing about this is that these operators will be really useful to work with regardless of which of the other coding languages you choose to use, whether you use C# or another alternative.

In this chapter, we'll look at the many sorts of operators and how to deal with them.

Arithmetic Operators in Action

When you're ready to start working with operators, the first one we'll go over is the arithmetic operators.

These will be rather straightforward to work with, and if you have taken any math courses in the past, you will have a solid understanding of how they function and will be able to work with them fairly quickly.

When we deal with some of these arithmetic operators, we'll discover that they're also in charge of instructing the computer to do some of these operations.

The arithmetic functions will work out the way we want as long as you remember the appropriate symbol, put the numbers in the right sequence, and utilize them correctly.

The following are some of the most common arithmetic operators that you may use with the C# language:

- "+" This is the operator for adding two numbers together.
  It is going to combine two operands.
  As a result, you'd obtain x+y=25.
- The subtraction operator is "-."
  It will enable you to subtract the right-hand operand's value from the left-hand operand's value. As a result, you'd obtain y-x=-5.
  This is the command that tells the computer to multiply the two operands. As a result, you may use x*y=150.
- "/" is the operator that tells the computer to divide the left and right operands. For instance, y/x.
- The residue of the modulo operator is commonly referred to as "percent."
  The left operand will be divided by the right operand, and the remainder will be returned.

The increment operator is "++." It is going to raise the operand's value by one. As a result, you'd get ++x=16 *"—" This is known as the decrement operator among programmers.

It is going to reduce the operand's value by one. As a result, you'll have —x=14.

You'll find that these arithmetic operators come in handy in a variety of situations, and they're rather simple to remember and utilize.

They may also be used in codes if you want to take two numbers or statements in the code and do some type of mathematical operation on them, such as addition or subtraction.

However, you must remember to utilize the sequence of operations with them to ensure that the code behaves as you like.

If you're unfamiliar with the order of operations and how it works, it's the approach that informs us in which order we need to have the numbers to execute the arithmetic properly and achieve the desired result.

Remember that we must complete all of the multiplication, then all of the division, then all of the addition, and lastly all of the subtraction from left to right. The solution will be incorrect if you do not utilize this while working in C#.

Assignment Operators in Action

Now that we've taken a closer look at the possibilities available with the arithmetic operators, it's time to move on to the second kind of operator that will perform well with C#: Assignment operators.

When we wish to assign a value to our variable or utilize another comparable approach, we'll use the assignment operators.

Consider the variables on which we've previously spent considerable time.

The variables, as well as other sections of our identifiers along the route, must be given a value.

Otherwise, you're merely reserving blank places in your computer's memory.

And the assignment operator will ensure that you can assign that value to it and that everything goes well.

The equal sign, as you would expect, is the most prevalent of these sorts of operators.

These operators are in charge of ensuring that the value is sent directly to the variable you choose.

However, some additional operators fall into this group that we may employ here.

Other assignment category operators you may know while working with this language and doing some of the coding's we'll look at later include:

- "=" You may use this operator to accomplish basic assignment operations. It will assign the value to a variable that you are currently working on.

  Writing int sample = 100, for example, tells the computer that you wish to assign 100 to the variable "sample."

  This variable or the value it contains will not be subjected to any further processing.
- The additive assignment operator is "+=". It will add the values of your two operands together and then assign the total to the left-hand operand.
- This is often referred to as the subtractive assignment operator by "-=" programmers.

  It will subtract the right-hand operand's value from the left-hand operand's value, then assign the difference to the left-hand operand.
- "*=" This operator multiplies the values of each operand before assigning the result to the left-hand operand.
- "/=" This is where you will divide the two variables and then assign the result to the left-hand variable.

When using one of the aforementioned assignment operators, be sure that both of your operands are the same type of data. Because the operands are different in certain circumstances, they will not be compatible with one another, and if you attempt to work with them, your program will not perform as you would expect. So, double-check this section of the code to ensure that you don't wind up with an issue that you'll have to correct later.

Relational Operators in Action

The relational operators are the next kind of operator on our list of operators.

Remember that the arithmetic operators we discussed earlier are in charge of assisting us in solving any mathematical equations we want within the codes, and the assignment operators are in charge of ensuring that all of our variables, or some of the spaces reserved in our computer's memory, have a good value assigned to them.

But now it's time to move our attention to the operation of these relational operators.

To begin, the relational operators will be the most useful since they will allow us to compare the values of two separate operands in the code.

These will be the ideal to employ when we handle some of our conditional statements later on since we can make this happen.

In this language, we may employ a variety of relational operators.

To make things simpler and to show what would happen when we apply them, we must assume that d = 100 and e = 150 from the start:

- "==" is the operator that can be used to check if two values are equal.

  The operand will tell you it is true if the two values are equal. Otherwise, the operand will inform you that it is incorrect. Saying d == e, for example, would result in a misleading result.

- "!=" This operator can be used to check if two values are equal.

  It will inform you this is true if the values are not equal.

  For example, true would be returned if e != d.

The operator ">" is used to see whether the operand on the left is larger than the operand on the right.

If it is, the operator will confirm that it is correct.

Saying that e > d is correct, for example.

- " This is the less than an operator, which allows you to see if the operand on the left is less than the operand on the right. If it is, such as the formula de, you will be able to make it seem true.

- ">=" is an operand that indicates whether the value of the operand on the left side is greater than or equal to the value of the operand on the right side.

Otherwise, it will inform you that the assertion is incorrect.

Saying that e >=d evaluates to true, for example.

If the operand on the left side is less than or equal to the operand on the right side, you'll obtain a true result with this operator.

For instance, d = e is correct.

When using this sort of operator, one thing to keep in mind is that you will always get a Boolean response.

This implies that depending on the criteria you apply to that section of the code, you will receive a true or false response.

It's a good idea for us to look through the code now and double-check that we've included the correct amount of equal signs to make this work. If we're using the equality operator, we'll need two equal signs; otherwise, we'll be using the assignment operator, which will give us a different result than what we're looking for right now.

The Logical Operators in Action

We can look at the next sort of operator, known as logical operators, which is vital for part of our work.

This one, like some of the other Boolean values, will accept and then depend on the concept of true and false when working with them in our code.

When we look at some of the logical operators that you may want to use in your code, we'll mostly concentrate on four options.

We'll look at them in more detail later, but to make things simpler, imagine that c and d are true and e is false:

The logical AND operator is denoted by the symbol "&&."

If both operands are true, the outcome will be true.

D && c, for example, will evaluate it as true.

- The logical AND operator is denoted by the symbol "&&."
  If both operands are true, the outcome will be true.
  D && c, for example, will assess it as true.

- "||" denotes a logical OR.
  If at least one of your operands is true, this operator will return a true result. True will be returned if c || e is used.

- "-this is the Logical Exclusive OR operator, and it returns true if one of the operands is true. The operator will return a false if both operands may be false or true.

- "!" -you can use this one to reverse the value of your Boolean variable. If you type in!d, for example, you'll receive a false.

Bitwise Operators in Action

Now it's time to move on to the last operator we'll cover in this handbook, the bitwise operators.

This is a form of the operator that, at first appearance, seems to be the same as the logical operators we've previously discussed.

The key difference between these bitwise operators and the preceding logical operators is that the bitwise options will only accept a binary value and then convert it to a Boolean result.

They are going to be values that indicate true or false, but they'll come out as a 0 or 1, and then we'll see these as the process's output.

Because many non-programmers will not grasp how these are meant to operate in some of the programs that they wish to develop, these binary values will be tough to deal with in general.

Let's look at an example of some of the various bitwise operators that may be used to see how they can be used in this context.

Let's assume that l = 0, h = 1, j = 0, and g = 1 *"&" is the Bitwise AND operator.

It will assign 1 to the places when both operands have a value of 1.

g & h, for example, will give you 1.

- The Bitwise AND operator is denoted by the symbol "&."
  It will assign 1 to the places when both operands have a value of 1.
  g & h, for example, will give you 1.
- "|" denotes a bitwise OR. When at least one of the operands has a 1 in it, it will assign 1 to the places. For example, typing h | 1 will return a result of 1.
- "" This is the only OR that will work with binary data.

When it comes to the various operators that we may use, the bitwise operator will need a little more effort.

And there aren't many occasions when we'd want to use this kind of operator in the programs we're writing.

However, this is an excellent alternative to work with and be aware of so that we can understand how it will function when we need it.

All of these types of operators will be useful in the programs we'll be writing along the road.

They're all a little different and can handle things differently as you go, but they can still help you get a lot done and see some solid outcomes in the code you're writing.

Take some time to go through them and discover how they function so you can quickly and easily include them in your code.

Chapter 5:

Using C# to teach your programs to make decisions

It's time to dive into some of the more exciting aspects of building our code in this chapter.

We'll learn a little more about conditional statements, also known as decision control statements, and how to make them work for our requirements. There are several occasions when we must design software that requires user input.

We can't always predict what kind of input the user will provide us. So, we can utilize these conditional statements and build up a condition for how we want them to react to various possible inputs, and then have the program behave appropriately depending on these conditions.

When you're working with your programs, you may want to make sure that they can make certain decisions on their own. You may set everything up ahead of time, with the correct circumstances, and then the code will react depending on the human input it gets. Even if you have no clue what the input is, the computer program will respond in the way you want it to, without you having to make a lot of assumptions.

You'll see that there are a few various sorts of conditional statements you may use, and the one you choose will be determined by how you want the code to behave. Each of these conditional expressions will enable us to function in a variety of circumstances, but the number of features and amount of decision-making you want the program to accomplish will vary. We'll look at a few of them throughout this chapter so you can understand what we're talking about and how everything will fit together.

As previously stated, we have more than one sort of conditional statement to pick from, and each may treat the information it receives as an input differently. This allows us to ensure that the code makes the correct judgment, regardless of how the user delivers information. Within our C# language, we have the following conditional statement options:

Conditional Statement If

The if statement is where we begin our trip into the realm of conditional statements.

This will be considered one of the most basic of all the conditional statements, and you will see that it occasionally lacks the functionality that we want in these statements.

Although we will not use the if conditional statement on its own very often, it does provide us with some experience with how it works and what we can do with it, so we will spend some time here. When we're ready to construct one of these if statements, we need to make sure that the code will only need to send a certain response to the user if the input fits all of the requirements that you provided in the code, to begin with. If the input meets the requirements, the code will run and, in most cases, the user will get some kind of notification. If this works better for your sort of programming, you may also have it go through and run something else. When we utilize the if statement, we only get a response or an output if the program's input fits the criteria in the code. The code will not run the following section of the code if the user provides incorrect input depending on the circumstances.

If a statement can detect whether the condition is satisfied or not, it doesn't have another portion of the code to inform it how to act. It will not execute the message or the section you added since it is not met. The good news is that configuring the if statement is a lot simpler than you would believe at first.

Examining the code sample provided below is a useful approach to check whether the statement may be used:

If (x > 0), then

{ \sConsole.

Write("The value is positive."); Write("The value is negative."); Write("The value is negative."); Write(

Certain things must occur in the scenario we just described.

If the user enters a figure that is more than zero, the software is programmed to output "The value is positive."

If the expression is found to be false or the input is less than zero, the computer will disregard the whole sentence following Console.

I'm going to write and then move on.

The If-Else Condition

As we reviewed in the preceding section, there are a few complications that might arise when working with the if statement.

Even as a novice, there are several scenarios in coding when they will be tough to utilize and won't get the job done that we desire.

For example, in our scripts, it is typically not a good idea to include the possibility that the computer would not operate at all if the input is incorrect.

You want to make sure that no matter what the user enters as input, even if the code you're dealing with considers it incorrect, some form of result will appear to let them know they've made a mistake or some other indicator.

The decision you make here will be based on the performance of your code.

This is why we'll take a break here and look at the second kind of conditional statement we might employ in our programs. The if-else statement is what it's called.

This will give your code a lot of strength, and it will allow us to have two, three, or even more possibilities to base the user's input on. You may potentially use as many of these choices as you like in the if statement, but the point is that it's set up in a way that ensures that everything receives a response. The following is a nice syntax to utilize to help us understand how the if-else expression works: If (the Boolean expression) If (the Boolean expression) If (the Boolean expression) If (the Boolean expression) If (the Boolean expression) If (the Boolean expression) If (the Boolean expression)

Else

If the result is false, the statement(s) you wish to execute;

As we can see from the code above, the if-else statement provides a great deal of flexibility.

When it comes to utilizing the if-else statement, this will be the most basic choice, but it's easy to expand it by adding additional lines and conditions to get the power you need.

Whether the response is false, the code simply bypasses the first condition and moves on to the second to determine if it is true or not.

If there are more than two possibilities, the procedure repeats itself until the else statement is reached. If the input does not fit the other parts of the statement, it will automatically match the else section of the statement, and the condition is satisfied.

That section of the code will run for us to guarantee that something appears on the screen at some point throughout the process. Now that we know a little bit more about how the if-else statement is meant to function for us, let's take a closer look at how it works with a real example to confirm that it acts the way we want it to. The following is an example of how we might apply this:

If (x > 0), then

"This value will be positive."); Console.Write("This value will be positive.");

If that fails, Console.Write("The value is less than or equal to zero.")

You'll see that in the previous example, the otherwise clause remains concealed, at least until the Boolean expression turns out to be false.

It will be present when and if the process demands it, or if the value for that case turns out to be untrue. However, if the result is true and meets the criteria you add to the code, you'll see that the first statement is the one we'll utilize. There may be many scenarios in which you will want to use the if-else statement in your C# code, but it may seem to be a little complicated to deal with as a novice.

Take some time to practice some of the codes we've included above to ensure that you get some practice typing them in and that they line up with how you wish to create your codes.

Nested Conditional Statements

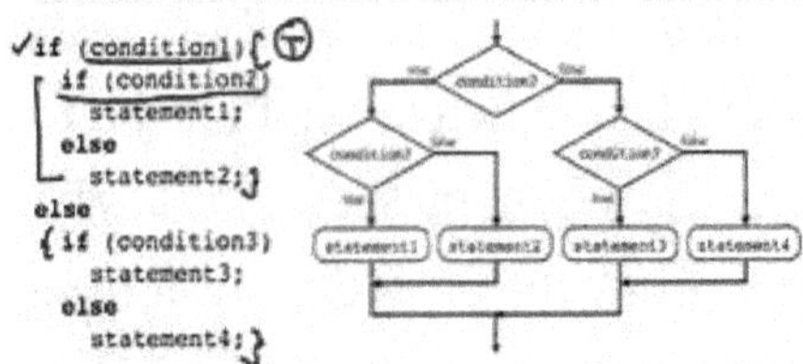

These are a kind of conditional statement that is nested inside another
The concept of nested conditional statements is a little different when working with conditional statements in C#.

These are where we'll combine two of the previous statements to form a nested conditional statement.

As a result, we may take one of our if statements and nest it within another if expression.

This will add a layer of complexity to what we're doing in our statements and may help us make our programs work even harder.

If this is the kind of conditional statement you want to work with, keep in mind that if you create one and make an error or a mistake, fixing it will take a long time.

Whether the issue occurs in the beginning, end, or anywhere in between, if it exists, it will produce an error throughout the code, and you must take the time to correct it or the code will not function.

This takes time and might be irritating for a newcomer trying to figure out how to do it.

Another thing to keep in mind with these nested conditional statements is that you can potentially go back and add as many layers to this one as you like.

As a novice, though, it's usually better not to go above three levels, and two is frequently plenty for the codes you wish to type down. If you use more than three tiers of conditional statements, you may wind up with code that is more difficult to manage and that does not perform as expected.

As a newbie, this is a nice guideline to follow to make coding a little simpler.

While this may seem complicated, and you may believe that your scripts would never require these nested statements, there are certain scenarios when they will, and it is an interesting bit of programming to understand whether or not you use it.

The following is an example of how to use the nested conditional statement to construct smart code:

60; 70; 60; 60; 60; 60; 60; 60; 60; 60; 60; 60; 60; 60; 60; 60

If (r ==s), then

System.Console.WriteLine("These numbers are equal. ");
System.Console.WriteLine("These numbers are equal. ");

Otherwise, if (r > s),

If not, System.Console.WriteLine("The value of the first variable is larger than the value of the second variable.")' Else, System.Console.WriteLine("The value of the second variable is more than the value of the first variable.")'

There are a few solutions that will work with the if-else clause in the example above.

This allows you to choose the command so that the software knows what to readout.

This will allow you to accomplish more with your software while also making it easy to make it more complex.

You'll want to use conditional statements in your C# code for a variety of reasons.

These will allow you to increase the amount of interaction between your code and the people who are using your software.

It's easy to use, yet it ensures that you can write sophisticated code in your software.

Chapter 6

Creating Objects in C#

C# is classified as an OOP language.

This indicates we're dealing with an object-oriented programming language, one whose structure will be centered on objects and classes.

This will be a basic issue that we can manage and deal with, but it is also necessary to learn more about it and understand why it is important, as well as what it means for some of the scripts that we will attempt to handle along the road.

The organization that we wish to retain and depend on inside the C# language will be unachievable without these classes and the objects that they contain.

This is why we need to learn more about OOP languages and why we will spend some time looking at the essential processes to assist us to construct these classes and objects in our code.

Let's delve in and see what we can make of it all.

Classes and Objects in C#

To help us get started on all of this, the first step is to spend some time discussing what objects are and how the C# language will utilize them to run code.

Programming has seen significant modifications since its inception, ensuring that programmers will use a variety of approaches to assist them to produce some of the new applications that their programs and computers need.

The object-oriented programming, or OOP, that we are discussing with C# and other comparable languages is one of the finest additions to these programming languages.

Most current coding languages will depend on this since it guarantees that your coding is simple to use and comprehend, and it will help us code better as beginners.

You will discover that there are several components that your coding must be able to manage to make a code operate.

However, the OOP component of our language will assist us in breaking all of these pieces down into more digestible chunks so that nothing is lost and everything behaves as it should.

We need to separate some of these components a little and then learn a bit more about what they are going to accomplish since there are a lot of things that need to work together to guarantee this process works and our application performs properly.

Let's take a look at the concept of these OOP languages, the classes, the objects, and everything else to see how it will function for us.

The Fundamentals of the OOP Language

When we arrive here, the first thing we need to grasp is what the OOP language means and why it is so vital to what we are doing in our coding. To put it simply, OOP is a coding style that is going to depend on objects, ones that are really produced by the programmer and can link back to some of the physical items that we see all the time in the world around us.

These OOP languages are useful because they can offer us the precise model we need to work with depending on how we want to utilize our objects, as well as how we want to deal with these things in the real world.

If you have a ball in your code, it will look, feel, and perform just as a ball would in the real world.

When compared to some of the other coding languages, you would have to spend more time on them dealing with more abstract notions.

Abstract notions are difficult to deal with, making it difficult for novices to grasp what was going on in the code, much alone apply it in a way that allowed them to code effectively.

This was the only way to accomplish things when coding first began, but it raised the bar too high for many individuals to enter the world of code, and most felt discouraged and gave up before they ever had a chance to begin.

The OOP languages, on the other hand, removed this hurdle and made things easy.

You get the advantage of getting rid of some of those abstract notions instead of having them set up such that you can deal with items that are simpler to handle and grasp.

And the majority of current coding languages now depend on this approach, which might make life simpler for you as a beginning.

The Items

Now that we've learned a little bit more about how these OOP languages are meant to operate and what they can do to make writing simpler for everyone, let's take a closer look at some of the objects that comprise this sort of language.

Programmers may interact with these items in any way they see fit.

These digital objects will be used to represent some of the real items that you wish to see in your code.

When working with any of the newer OOP languages, including C#, bear in mind that the objects must have a few important qualities to function properly.

These qualities will include:

- State—this is the feature that will define the item. These might be both generic and particular.
- Behavior—this is the property that declares all of the activities that an object is capable of.

Looking at an example of this is an excellent way to ensure that we have a better understanding of how things are supposed to operate.

Assume we want to add a ball to our code.

What the status of this ball will be.

Things like the material of the ball, the size of the ball, and the color of the ball.

We could even discuss how the ball feels in our hands.

When discussing the behavior of the ball, on the other hand, we would concentrate more on the things that the ball can accomplish.

This might involve things like the ball rolling, bouncing, kicking, and tossing the ball, among other things.

When we wish to deal with one of these languages, we will discover that it is simple to merge the information and the approach, and then we can process them as the same thing.

The programming object will then have time to match up to how it is meant to behave and appear in the real world, and it will go through and save all of this information and actions for later use when the code runs. These objects will be a crucial element of the code that we will develop. We'll be using a lot of objects along the road, and as we'll see in a minute, the classes we can design will come in and give us all of the storage we need, ensuring that these things remain together and are simple to discover at the proper portions of the code.

The Courses

The classes are the next item we need to look at about them.

While we're on the subject of looking at some of the objects and how they're meant to operate, it's time to go through and take a closer look at the classes and how they'll link to some of the things we deal with, as well as what this means for our coding language.

To begin, when we work with the C# language, the classes will be the component that helps define the features of the objects we created before and may help us keep all of them for organizational reasons.

These classes are useful because they will assist us in establishing a framework or model on which to build things, making it simpler to adequately specify the nature of any item that our classes are designed to store.

The classes will be regarded as part of the basis of what is required to make the OOP language function properly, and they will then be immediately connected back to the object that goes with it.

They will enable us to add as many pieces as we desire, sometimes even a collection, as long as they complement one another.

This takes us to the point where we'll need to dig a little further to understand how these classes will operate in our code.

The example that we will look at here will be a new class called Toys, and the object that we want to put into this particular class will be called Ball.

The ball will be only one of the instances of the Toy class that we are generating with this specific instance.

However, the Toy class will assist us with this one since it helps to specify the behavior and state of not just the object of the ball, but also any additional toys that we attempt to put into that class.

In addition to the ball, we may go through and insert items such as a bike, a doll, a dinosaur, or whatever else.

Our class might declare both of these objects at the same time.

How to Make a Class in C#

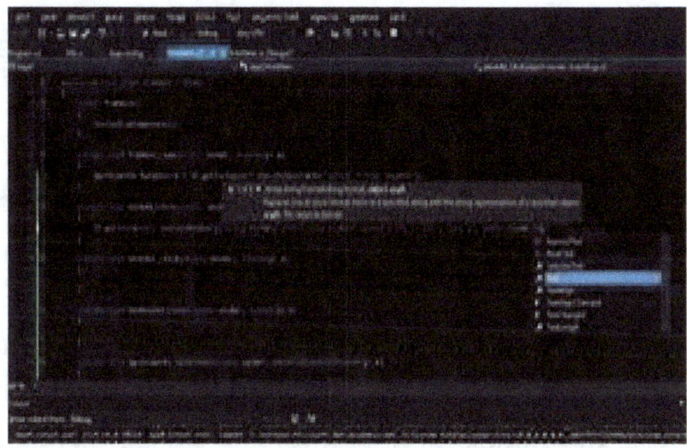

With some of the material we talked about previously, it is time to take things a step further and design one of our classes in this language.

After we've had a chance to work on some of our programs and added the "class" keyword, it's time to go through and tell the identifier what you want to see.

This must be done in conjunction with some of the variables and methods that you want to use for the class to function properly.

Of course, we want to get as much power behind this as feasible while making it as easy as possible.

To guarantee that this occurs, we must employ all of the necessary components and verify that they are in proper working condition.

When designing our classes, we must add the following components:

*Fields—these are any variables that will correspond to a certain data type.

*Techniques—these are the methods you can use to alter the data.

*Properties—in this language, the properties will improve how effectively the fields function.

The property will offer some additional management capabilities for the data and distribute it to the fields.

At this point, it will probably be simpler if you look at how to work with the classes and ensure that they accomplish what you want.

We'll now look at an example of how this code would operate and the many ideas that have been proposed about it.

In this case, we'll call the class "book," and it'll contain the characteristics of size and type.

As an example, consider the following:

Book of public classes

Private string BookType: Private string size; Public string BookType: Public string size

Get this and return it. BookType;

Set This. BookType = value'

Size of the public string

Obtain and return this size;

Specify this.size = value;

this.bookType = "Dictionary"; this.size = "big"; public Book()

this.bookType = bookType; this.size = size; public book(string bookType, string size)

void in public Sample()

{ \sConsole.WriteLine

"Is this a 0, BookType?"

Now that we've had some time to develop one of our classes, it's time to move on to developing some of our objects.

We need to populate some of the classes with these objects so that they have a function inside the code that we're developing here.

And that is precisely what we are going to do right now.

After we've gone through and created the classes mentioned above, it's time to go through and construct a few objects that will operate in our scripts and can be plugged directly into our classes.

Creating our objects will not be tough to work with, so we will take some time to look at all of the steps that we can take to make this happen, as well as what we can do to help generate an object, whether it is just one or many, for our code to operate.

With some of these notions in mind, the first thing we need to concentrate on here is learning how to build one of the essential objects inside one of the classes that we built earlier.

To assist us to get started, we'll need to go through and create a new keyword.

Typically, the programmer will begin by assigning a new object to their variable to verify that it becomes the same data type as the class you want it in.

Remember that doing so will not assist us to copy the object to the variable that we want to use, but it will be handy when we want the variable to have a reference to the object that we assigned to it.

Take a look at the code below to ensure that we understand how to achieve this:

Book someBook = brand-new Book ()

This is an excellent example to use since it will take the instance of a book and assign it to the variable we designated some book.

This ensures that the correct item is sent to the correct class.

Then we may look at some of the system's classes that will be useful for the task we're doing.

Sometimes with this language, a characteristic that we might appreciate is the library that comes with it.

This library will automatically contain many of the classes that you will require, such as the console, string, and math, so that we may use them as a default.

As you go through and create more of these routines, keep in mind that the.NET framework that comes with it is designed to operate well with the C# library, so utilizing it should be simple.

While we're on the subject, you'll fall in love with how simple it is to utilize the.NET framework to get the job done.

This is because the library you wish to utilize with the C# language will operate just well with this framework, and you will discover that they get along well and don't create too many problems.

These lessons that you utilize are beneficial as a novice, particularly if you have never worked with programming before.

One thing to keep in mind is that when you deal with these classes, they will go through the process of concealing the logical implementations.

You must continue to concentrate on what the lessons will accomplish for you rather than on the mechanics of how they will get the task done.

As a result, the classes that have been developed within the C# language will not be exposed to the public.

Simply browse through these programs and utilize them for general reasons rather than the mechanics of things.

Adding a Parameter to the Object

Another issue on which we should spend some time in the C# language is how to ensure that we supply the correct parameters to the object. This language will make it easy to provide parameters to any object, as long as it is one that you have previously built.

This is a really simple approach to use, and you may add arguments to any of the objects in your code.

The correct syntax that we may use to assign these parameters, or any other parameters that you like to the object, will be as follows:

Book some book = new Book("Biography", "big")'; This code will create a new object called some book and apply the two separate arguments to it.

The object's type has been changed to Biography, and its size has been increased to big.

When you use the new keyword, the.NET framework will do two things: It will set aside some memory for this new object.

It will initialize the data members of the object.

This is a simple operation owing to what is known as the constructor method.

The arguments that we were able to put forth for the code that we took the effort to generate above will be the same parameters that we would use for the class constructor.

This is there to guarantee that the object stays where it should in any of the classes we pick, and it is there to give an object with qualities that will allow the object to behave correctly in our code.

Objects Are Being Released

When we speak about releasing objects, we mean that we can release any objects that appear too often in our code, or that are large and may take up too much memory and processing power within the system, without having to go through and manually delete them along the way.

You may utilize one of the existing systems on the.NET framework to do this, and the CLR system is also a viable choice.

When you are ready to release some of the objects as required by the CLR system, the compiler will be configured to detect and then automatically release the objects.

The memory allocated in the code to deal with these things is now free, and you may add another object or variable to the memory space as long as you take the effort to construct it as well.

If you want to ensure that the object you choose is released, you must first understand how to delete the relevant reference to that object. Otherwise, this will not work.

To make all of this happen, we'll need to utilize the following code:
null some book = null

This operation will not destroy the object, but it will ensure that all references to that object are deleted so that the CLR can go through when you are through and delete it for you.

This is a fantastic procedure to have since it will assist to minimize the number of problems that emerge in your code and may eliminate some of the errors that appear.

As we can see, there are a variety of things we can put together to assist us with these classes and objects.

When we combine all of these, we can create a great robust code that performs well and has all of the various aspects that we need to be successful.

Chapter 7:

Creating C# Classes

We touched on these classes briefly in the last chapter, but largely in terms of how they would connect to our objects and make our programs stronger in that way.

Now it's time to take things a step further and get into these courses.

Working with these classes and the objects that go with them is one of the benefits of working with the C# language and the fact that it is considered an OOP language.

But, to guarantee that everything is correctly set up and that we can put things together and get them to function for our requirements, we must define the classes, call them up, and do several additional tasks.

That is precisely what this chapter is about.

Working with Our Students

When it comes time to include one of these classes in the C# language, the class must be done correctly.

This is significant because it will assist us in defining the sorts of objects and data types that we will utilize in that section of the program.

The object will assist us in containing the information that will eventually define the class, which can be seen as a sort of container in the code that our object is located inside.

These classes will be useful to work with since they have a lot of information that they can bring forward anytime we need it.

They can not only hold onto all of the items that we construct, but they can also hold onto any of the information that will explain the characteristics and behavior that come with these objects.

The behavior that we are discussing here is all of the behavior that we want the objects to manage while the code is executed.

When we deal with OOP languages like C#, you will see why it is critical to work with methods that can get the job done in this manner.

So, the first thing we need to do here is going through all of the crucial components that need to be present in our class.

There will be various components that are great to work with and should be there to ensure that the class behaves.

There are a few more components that we must consider while processing the classes, including the following:

- Declaration—this is the line that will declare the class's identifier.
- Body—just like methods, the classes will have a single body.

You must specify the body immediately after making the statement. The body is the statement (or statements) located between the curly brackets.

Here's an example: class Example /This is the body of the "Example" class.

Constructor—This is the component that allows you to create a new object. Public Sample() /Insert anything you want to say here is an example of this.

- Fields are the variables that will be declared inside your class. The fields will contain values that indicate the precise state of the object they are attempting to access. This section will cover the various characteristics of the class.
- Many programmers will write the class properties directly within the object's field.
- Methods—a method is essentially a named unit of executable code.

It may execute certain tasks before allowing objects to achieve the desired behavior. It can also run the appropriate algorithms included inside the programs.

When we go through and build some of the codes and classes that we want to utilize in this language, keep in mind that we are not able to go through and directly manipulate the things that we want to create. Instead, you will need to go through and assign the objects ahead of time so that you can handle some of the manipulations that you want to deal with later on without worrying about the complications.

How to Plan Your Classes

The second thing to consider is that we need to organize the classes that we are working on within the C# language.

There is primarily one major guideline that we must adhere to for these classes to function properly.

This guideline states that we must double-check that our classes have been saved. cs files.

This makes them much simpler to locate for us and the compiler, allowing the code to bring the class out at the appropriate moment.

If we look at it from a technical standpoint, the C# language can take all of our classes and store them in a program with a single large file name, and then the compiler can go through and read that information without encountering any issues.

However, many programmers prefer to keep their classes in separate files since it provides for the greater convenience of use while working on the individual files and may aid in organizing.

Both ways, however, are effective, so choose the one that appeals to you the most.

At this point, we must comprehend the concept of a namespace in code. This will be a collection of classes that are all connected in some way.

The manner they may connect will be determined by your code and the context you place them in, but there should be some reason as to why they relate to one another.

It might be anything as simple as their classes, interfaces, structure, or even the information contained inside them.

If you are creating the code and want to add or create a new namespace in some of the previous codes, you must work with the directive of "using" to make this easy.

However, it is generally preferable to perform this directly at the start of that section of code, in the first few lines, so that is an option as well.

Getting to Know Our Classes

The last issue we need to look at in this handbook is how to access one of our lectures in this language.

This language is special in that it will offer us four modifiers that we can use to help access our classes and even select who else can access them.

These four modifiers will include protected, public, private, and internal, and they will have the control needed to determine when the portions may be brought up, which parts of the code can bring them up, and more.

Below is further information on how each of these modifiers works:

- **Private:** This is the modification that will impose severe limitations on one of your classes. If the class is marked as private, the other classes in the code will not be able to access it. If you don't put anything else there, the C# language will take this as the default modifier. This might help you prevent issues if you fail to include that modification.
- **Public:** You have the option of making the class public.
  This implies that the modifier informs other classes that they may use this class.
  This modification will remove any restrictions on how visible this class is to the rest of the classes.
- **Internal:** If your code contains the internal modifier, it signifies that this class will be available, but only to files in the same project.
- **Protected:** This is the modification you'll use if you don't want a user to be able to access the element.However, it also enables all descendant classes to have access to that class's components if necessary.

As you can see with this one, all of the pieces may operate in somewhat various ways depending on what you want to see happen within some of your programs.

You may decide if a certain section, or all of it, needs to remain secret, or whether it can be made public for others to view.

You can select whether or not anything will be protected.

It all depends on the kind of code you're attempting to write and what you want to happen with all of the classes you build.

When working with the C# language, we can develop a lot of amazing classes, and these classes, along with the objects that go inside of them, are one of the nicest aspects that come with this language.

Learning how to work with them and what they can do for some of the programs we want to create can be fairly remarkable, and we can accomplish so much with these classes along the road.

Chapter 8:

How to Make a C# Loop

Now that we have a better idea of how classes and objects will operate in some of our programs, it is time to delve in a little deeper and look more closely at another subject that will help our codes come to life in no time.

Many of the OOP languages that we want to spend our time on will allow us to work with a sort of coding that is easy, can tidy up the code, and can let fairly intricate sections of our coding be done in just a few lines, and these are known as loops.

As previously said, these loops will be quite useful.

They save us a lot of time and trouble in the process, and they may guarantee that the whole process of writing out programs does not take as long as it used to.

In this chapter, we'll take a look at what these loops are like, how we can make them, and even some of the alternatives we have when it comes to employing loops for our requirements.

When we discuss loops in any coding language, we can think of them as a method that is used to help us execute a statement, or in some cases, a set of statements, many times over and over again, depending on the results of the condition that we put in place and that we want the loop to be able to evaluate in the first place.

Depending on how the program works and what we want to gain out of it in the process, the loop may just go through the iteration a few times, or it may go through it many times.

In many circumstances, we will discover that the loops we wish to deal with are classified into two types.

The first kind will be called as entry controlled loops.

The loops in which the condition is verified at the beginning of the loop will thereafter be part of these entry regulated loops.

There are a few possibilities here, including the while loop and the for loop.

In order for us to really understand how this is meant to operate, we must ensure that whatever condition you are testing appears at the beginning of the code.

The compiler will first verify the condition contained in the syntax, and if it finds it to be true, it will perform the loop.

This will work fine for the majority of the loops we wish to deal with, but there will be certain cases when the loop will not execute at all because the requirements are not satisfied.

To assist us out, let's take a closer look at a couple of the loops that fall into this category.

The first kind will be referred to as a while loop.

The test condition will be visible right at the beginning of the loop with this one, and then all of the statements that we may work with will be performed until the provided condition, which is the Boolean in these loops, can be met.

When the condition we're dealing with is recognized as false with this one, the control will be removed from the while loop, and the loop will have to come to a full stop.

Instead of performing the loop at all, it will go to the next section of code. Working with this kind of code and loop is not difficult.

In a minute, we'll take a look at an example of how we might manage this.

Take a look at the syntax and play about with it a little to understand how it works.

You can also check for the while section of the code, which will tell us where the loop we're dealing with will begin.

The following is an example of how we may use the while loop:

```
/ C# application to demonstrate a while loop using System;
whileLoopDemo is a class.
public static void Main() int x = 1; / Exit when x is larger than 4
while (x = 4)
Console.WriteLine("GeeksforGeeks"); / Increment the value of x for the
next iteration x++;
```

When it comes to constructing this kind of loop, one that is set up to write out a certain message three times, we use a while loop that tells our code to only do this three times and no more.

If we had set up the loop to execute this four times, the condition we're dealing with would be interpreted as false, and we'd get the erroneous results.

This code will see that we are true when we write it out once since it is less than four times.

The same holds true when we increase the numbers and have them printed out twice, then three times.

But when the loop runs again, it will conduct that last iteration and notice that if it writes it again, it will do it the fourth time, which will also fail.

It is also possible to go through and alter some of the phrases that we want to perform with this kind of loop, and discover which statements work best for your coding here.

You can also acquire some experience by fiddling about a little and changing around the iterations and more to see if it still works the way you want it to.

When you've finished playing with that section of the code, it's time to move on and work with the for loop.

This will be similar to the functions we saw in the while loop, but the syntax will be different since the way this operates is different.

When the number of times you want the loop's statement to run is known ahead of time, for loops are one of the best strategies to use.

When we initialize our loop variable, or the condition that we want to test, and the decrement or increment of the variable is done with just a single line for the loop, we know that we are dealing with something that offers us a structure that is shorter and simpler to work with for our loop. And if you run into issues or want to be able to modify certain areas of your code, you may discover that it is simpler for us to format the loops so that they may be debugged afterwards.

Now, before we dive into this for loop any further, we need to look at a number of the key components of this process to verify that the loop behaves in the way that we want it to.

The actions that we may take here are as follows:

1. Create the variable that will be used for the loop:
    To start things moving, the expression that controls the loop, also known as the variable, must first be initialized. This is going to be the starting point for this loop. You may utilize an existing defined variable, or you can declare a local variable in the loop we're presently in.
2. Include the condition for testing: The second aspect of this procedure that we need to look at is the condition for testing.
    This is the section where we may execute all of the statements contained in the loop. It will be utilized in a variety of circumstances to assist us in testing the condition for leaving the loop.
    We must ensure that it delivers a Boolean value, i.e. a result that is either true or false. When the condition is false, the loop is finished.
3. The increments and decrements:
    The variable of the loop will be either incremented or decremented depending on what we want to get out of it and the control that we put in. When this is ready to happen in either way, we will be able to return to our testing conditions to verify whether everything matches up or if it is time to end the loop at this point.

Before we go through the process of looking at some of the codings that we want to do with this, keep in mind that the initialization section will only be evaluated once before the for loop begins.

If you put it up in the way that you want to view it, this will be more than plenty.

With this in mind, let's add some of the information we discussed above to the program to see how this kind of loop would work
/ C# application to demonstrate a loop.

using System; class forLoopDemo public static void Main() / for loop starts at x=1 / and continues until x =4 for (int x = 1; x = 4; x++) Console. WriteLine("GeeksforGeeks");

As previously stated, the two loops we just went through will be referred to as entry-controlled loops in this language.

But now it's time to look at another kind of loop that we may use in our code, and these are known as exit-controlled loops.

This kind of category includes loops in which the testing condition is located towards the conclusion of the loop's body.

One thing to keep in mind about these loops is that they will be reviewed at least once.

The code will go through the loop, then look for the testing conditions to determine whether they exist before running through the loop again.

These criteria will not be discovered at the start of the code.

With this in mind, let's take a look at the do-while loop, which is one of the most popular loops in this category. There will be many situations in the C# language when we will wish to deal with the do-while loop. However, you may see some parallels with the while loop that we discussed before.

The primary distinction between the while loop and the do-while loop is that the do-while loop is designed to verify the conditions after the statements have been performed.

What we mean is that it will do the process of running our loop once, and then it will be able to verify the criteria to see whether they have been satisfied or not, rather than having this all happen at the start. Using this in mind, let's go through some of the work that we can accomplish with the syntax of the do-while loop. These are excellent loops to work with, and they will supply us with a plethora of useful routines in the process.

Take a look at the code below to understand what's going on and what components appear when we wish to establish a do-while loop.

```
/ C# application demonstrating a do-while loop using System; class dowhileloopDemo

int x = 21; do public static void Main();
/ The line will be printed twice.
If the condition is false, Console is invoked.
WriteLine("GeeksforGeeks"); x++; while (x 20);
```

When working on our C# loops, we have another option available to us called endless loops.

These are one-of-a-kind, and they essentially have the test condition not evaluating anything as false at any moment.

This means that the loop will get stuck and will continue to run the statement you have there indefinitely.

To get this cycle to halt, you'll need to apply some external force. This is generally what happens when you're working on the loop and forget to include some of the requirements that are required for it to perform properly. You must go over this and add the correct conditions from the start, as well as ensuring that everything is in the right location, so that you do not wind up with an endless loop that you are trapped with along the way.

With this in mind, we must examine this loop to discover what it is capable of. It will appear similar to some of the loops we created before, but there will be a few variations, which is what will make it one of these endless loops in the first place. An endless loop may be used in the following ways:

/ A C# application that uses System to show an endless loop.
class infiniteLoop public static void Main() / The statement will be written
/ indefinitely (;;)
Console.
WriteLine("This is printed an unlimited number of times");

In certain cases, while writing your code, you may discover that combining two loops, and occasionally more, is the most beneficial to the task at hand.

If this is the case with your code, you should ensure that you can combine the loops and have them run until they are finished. This will be useful in a variety of sorts of scripts, whether we're dealing with a multiplication table or something simple. A nice example of code that you may use to create one of these loops is as follows:

/ C# application demonstrating nested loops with System; class
nestedLoops public static void Main() / loop inside loop printing
GeeksforGeeks for(int I = 2; I 3; i++) for(int j = 1; j I j++)
WriteLine("GeeksforGeeks");

And now we get to the last form of loop that we may look at in this chapter.

This last loop will be referred to as the continue statement.

This is a handy statement since it is meant to jump to the execution phase of the loop if a certain condition is fulfilled, and then it will change the flow so that it is on the next part for updating when we want.

This one is sometimes difficult to describe, so let's have a look at some of the codings below to help us get a better concept of how the continue statement should appear and work:

/ C# application to show the continue statement using System; class demonstration

Continue public static void Main() / GeeksforGeeks is printed just twice / due to the continue statement for(int I = 1; I 3; i++) if(i == 2) continue;

Console.WriteLine("GeeksforGeeks")

When it comes to bringing in these loops and making them work for some of our requirements along the route, you have a lot of options. Each code that you write will be somewhat different from the others, so it is always a good idea to spend some time and learn about these loops, how each one will function in some of the codings that we want to develop, and how they can save us time while keeping our code tidy and organized along the way.

(Chapter 9)

Arrays, Lists, and Strings

```java
public static boolean contains(ArrayList<Integer> list, int value) {
    return contains(list, value, 0);
}

private static boolean contains(ArrayList<Integer> list, int value, int idx) {
    boolean hasInt = false;

    if (idx < list.size()) {
        if (list.get(idx) == value) {
            hasInt = true;
        } else {
            hasInt = contains(list, value, idx + 1);
        }
    }

    return hasInt;
}
```

In this chapter, we'll look at a few of the most significant aspects of working with the C# language to help fill out the information we've gained so far. In this chapter, we'll look at three crucial components of our coding language that are comparable and kind of go together, so we'll group them.

We'll be working with arrays, lists, and strings, and although they may seem to be quite similar, some key distinctions will show up in your code. Strings, lists, and arrays will be used extensively in many of the C# programs you build. And which one you choose will frequently be determined by what you want to accomplish with your code, as well as what you hope to see the items and lists you create do in the long run.

So, with that in mind, let's look at some of the similarities and differences between strings, lists, and arrays; some of the code that can be done with them; and more to get us started.

Making Use of Strings

```
1  string sentence = "Hi there"; // Defining a string to turn to characters
2
3  char[] charter = sentence.ToCharArray() // turns string to a list of characters.
4
5  //The output of charter would be:
6  //[ 'H', 'i', ' ', 't', 'h', 'e', 'r', 'e' ]
7
8
9  /*
10  Compiled by Sam Kimbone
11  */
```

The first aspect of this procedure that we must devote some effort to is the strings. To keep things simple, a string is one of the C# objects that may contain a text value. Internally, the text will be saved as a sequential and read-only collection of char objects. When we utilize this kind of string, there is no chance of a character for null terminating, which implies that the string may have as many embedded null characters as you like. Along with this, we must consider the fact that the length property of our string is significant here, as it might reflect the number of char objects discovered in the string.

This implies that when we speak about strings, we must consider the number of char objects present rather than the Unicode letters. If you want to go through and access all of the individual code points that are considered Unicode and are in a certain string, you must use the StringInfo object.

Now, before we go any further, we need to look at something that will appear in some of your programs. You should observe that there is an item known as a string and another portion known as System. String. The string keyword is essentially an alias for String that we use whenever we deal with C#.

This implies that String and string will be the same, and you may use whatever naming scheme you wish to make this work. However, as we go through this, you will see that the String class is unusual in that it provides the programmer with all of the methods required to edit, produce, and even compare the different sorts of strings in our code. This language may even overload some of our operators to make working with basic string operations simpler. Keeping things in order and ensuring that we deal with strings correctly, whether we utilize them for operations or not, is critical in most of the code we do. Now that we have all of this information, it is time to look at the code that we can use to first define, and then initialize, the string that we are wanting to work with. There are numerous approaches we may use to do this, and we'll look at a number of them below:

/ Declare but do not initialize.

string message1; / Set to null.

string message2 = null; / Begin with an empty string.

/ Instead of the literal ", use the Empty constant.

message3 string = System

String.

Empty; / Begin with a standard string literal.

string oldPath = "c:Program FilesMicrosoft Visual Studio 8.0"; / Begin with a literal string.

@string newPath "c:Program Files (x86)

Visual Studio 9.0 (Microsoft) "; / Make use of System.

If you prefer, use string.

System.

String greeting = "Hello World!"; / You may use implicit typing in local variables (i.e. inside a method body).

var temperature = "I'm still a System with a powerful type.

'String!' "; / Use a const string to avoid'message4' being used to hold another string value.

const string message4 = "You can't get rid of me!"; / Only use the String constructor when constructing a string from a char*, char[, or sbyte*. For further information, see the / System. String documentation.

letters = char[] 'A', 'B', 'C';

alphabet string = new string(letters);

Making a List

```
1  (double, int) t1 = (4.5, 3);
2  Console.WriteLine($"Tuple with elements {t1.Item1} and {t1.Item2}.");
3  // Output:
4  // Tuple with elements 4.5 and 3
5
6  (double Sum, int Count) t2 = (4.5, 3);
7  Console.WriteLine($"Sum of {t2.Count} elements is {t2.Sum}.");
8  // Output:
9  // Sum of 3 elements is 4.5
10
```

Following that, we may look at the lists.

These will be vital to deal with when it comes to our aims with the C# language, and they will be found in a variety of other coding languages as well.

Essentially, the list is simply an object that will accept your variables and hold them in the order that you choose.

The kind of variable that the list may hold will be specified using a relatively broad syntax, to begin with, but we can go through and add items as we go.

When we first start, the list and the array will seem to be quite similar, but as you work with them, you will find a few distinctions that we must keep in mind.

First, the list may be dynamically sized, but the array must have a fixed size that you provide at the start.

When you are unsure about how many variables to include or if you need any at all, a list is preferable since it allows you to make more adjustments to it.

Furthermore, when you add things to one of these lists, you may make modifications to them.

You can't go through and edit the things that are put within using a few other possibilities, such as the tuple or the array.

With a list, however, if you feel the need to vary things around and not have them all be the same, even though the execution of the program will still be something we can play with.

You'll discover that the list in this language is something you may utilize daily to get work done in your coding. You may discover that with these lists, you may add as many different things as you need, move them around, make revisions, and so much more. A smart approach to thinking about the list is similar to the one you create before going grocery shopping. You can write on it a lot, make modifications, shift stuff around, and do other things.

This is how the list can also operate with this language.

Finally, the Arrays

In addition to working with the strings and lists stated before, it is now time to look at C# arrays and how they function. We may use the array to create a set of variables and store them all as long as they are of the same data type. You will be able to define the array with which you want to operate by describing the type of its elements. So, if you want the array to hold one of the items, independent of which one we bring up, we must provide the object as its type.

Before we take the time to write out some of the code that will help us construct some of the arrays that we desire, it is crucial to understand what an array is and why we want to deal with it in general.

An array will have numerous attributes that we may utilize, some of them will be as follows:

1. When we utilize an array, we may choose between single-dimensional, multidimensional, or jagged arrays.

2. The dimensions and length that you will see in our array with these dimensions will be determined when you initially construct the array instance.
These are settings that we will be unable to modify after we create it, regardless of how long we decide to utilize the instance overall.

3. The default values that we can see with the elements of a numerical array will begin with zero, and when we interact with the elements that are part of the reference, they will be null.

4. When dealing with an array that seems jagged, keep in mind that it is an array of arrays.
This implies that all of the individual components we'll be using are reference types, and they'll be initialized when we get to null.

5. We must also keep in mind that the arrays will be indexed at zero.
What this means for our code is that the array will begin with 0 as the first element and end with n-1 as the final member.

6. The various components that we may locate in our array can be of any kind that we choose depending on our code.
They may even be of the array variable.

7. The array types that we will be dealing with here will be reference types that we will be able to derive from the abstract base type known as Array.

Now, you'll see that you'll need to bring in these arrays quite a few times while working on some of the C# code you wish to write. And knowing how to work with them and what they can accomplish for the programs you wish to develop will be essential. That is why it is important to grasp some of the above-mentioned properties so that we may investigate some of the various portions of the code that we can accomplish with these arrays below.

When it comes to constructing our arrays in the C# programming language, we have numerous options.

Based on the codes that we are dealing with, the code that we will look at below is useful since it is set up to enable us to work with multiple distinct arrays, including the jagged array, the multidimensional array, and the single-dimensional array.

We will be able to accomplish the following using this one's code:

```
static void Main class TestArraysClass ()
/ Create a one-dimensional array.
/ Declare and set array element values. int[] array1 = new int[5];
array2 = new int[] 1, 3, 5, 7, 9; / Alternate syntax.
int[,] multiDimensionalArray1 = new int[2, 3]; / Declare and set array
element values. int[,] multiDimensionalArray2 = new int[2, 3]; / Declare
and set array element values.
int[,] multiDimensionalArray2 = 1, 2, 3, 4, 5, 6; / Create a jagged array.
jaggedArray = new int[6][] int[6][] int[6][] int[6][] int[6][] int[
; / Initialize the first array in the jagged array structure.
jaggedArray[0] = new int[4] 1, 2, 3, 4;
```

Strings, lists, and arrays in the C# language may add a new level to some of the work that we are attempting to do, and we must take the time to understand how to include them into our routines. We can see that each one will be a little different, and it frequently relies on what we want to get out of the process as well as how we want the code to behave. Take some time to examine these three possibilities and discover how they interact with one another, how they vary, and how we may utilize them in our code.

Chapter 10:

Tips and Tricks for Making the Most of C#

This handbook has spent some time going over all of the various aspects of coding that we need to know in order to use the C# language to develop some of our own code. When it comes to working on this language, there are a lot of various factors that we need to keep in mind, but once we get it all together, we'll discover that we can build some excellent codes and programs in the process.

Even though many of the latest coding languages available have been intended to make programming simpler for novices, there will be some hurdles that you will face when you first begin. It will be critical to discover the correct tips and methods to assist us learn this language and ensure that we can latch on to the various components fast and effectively.

One thing that a novice must remember while going through this process is that they must practice and learn from their errors as well as some of the difficulties that arise in their coding.

Even taking a break will help you get started on this and guarantee that you don't burn out and have problems with the procedure later on.

This chapter will look at the many elements of the coding that we can accomplish using C#, as well as some of the greatest ideas and recommendations that will guarantee we can do as much as possible with some of our own coding choices along the road. When you first start coding in a new language, there is a lot to learn, and it is critical to understand how to make it as user-friendly as possible. When it comes to dealing with the C# language, some of the ideas and recommendations that you may follow include:

Get Plenty of Practice

The first suggestion we may follow while learning the C# language is to gain a lot of practice.

There are a lot of codes, recommendations, and things to learn about in this handbook, but until you open up the compiler with C# and test some of it out, you will never obtain the skills and more that you need to truly make this work for you.

That is why the first guideline we must follow is to experiment with the code and get as much experience as possible.

The sooner we can get our hands dirty and start mucking about with the code on any new topic that we want to investigate and learn about in any coding language, the quicker we can really understand some of the principles that are there. You can't go through and read the material without utilizing it and then expect to retain it and be able to use the code in your own projects.

You must experiment with the code to discover how it works.

Now, you'll notice that the simplest approach to get started with this tip is to just open up our C# compiler and begin writing some of the code that we want right away. Take some of the examples in this manual and play around with them a little.

Even just putting them into the compiler to begin with is a solid step in the right direction and will allow us to get some experience. From there, you may work and experiment to achieve the best outcomes.

The Basics Are Your Friend

Another thing to think about is how to master some of the principles of our coding language.

Even though the foundations seem to be too simple to deal with at times, and you may feel as if you should simply sprint through them without a second thought, it is still necessary to spend time understanding about how they operate.

As simple as they are, they are also quite crucial to deal with. The better we become at these basics, the simpler it will be to grasp some of the more complex material that will come along. Those programmers who strive to get into a programming language and then hurry through the initial sections, failing to spend enough time on some of the foundations, will be the first to become stuck when it comes time to shift into some of the advanced stuff that will follow. So, before you miss some of the initial lessons that we need and skip over some of the fundamentals that are vital in all of this, be sure to learn more about the fundamentals and what we can do with them along the road.

Make a note of it.

It is natural to want to get started with programming by just opening the compiler and performing all of the code there.

And, although this is one option to attempt, sometimes trying it in a new way, and writing it by hand rather than typing it in all the time, will be the secret that will help us get this done.

Using a pen and paper to jot down our codes will assist.

There have been several advancements in computer technology, and there are numerous advantages to utilizing them. However, sometimes the greatest approach to learn anything new is to write it down and proceed from there. Whether you use scrap paper, a notepad, a whiteboard, or another method, spending the time to code everything out by hand will take more time to work with. There is a necessity to employ greater care, accuracy, and even purpose behind any lines of code that you attempt to create.You also can't check out the code as easily as you can on a computer, so you have to pay more attention. When it comes time to get things done, this strategy will take more time and be more time consuming. But it will be a terrific approach for us to go through and become better developers as a result. And, whether you want to use this in college or for a new career, being able to write down the codes that you are utilizing and apply this for your purposes will be critical to your success. The more time and effort you put into handwriting some of your codes, the better you will get at comprehending the coding and all that it can achieve. It requires the programmer to slow down and concentrate on what they want the scripts to perform. Then you may use it to detect your own errors and discover what works best for you and what does not.

Seek Assistance

When we initially start creating programs in this fashion, we may have a lot of lofty notions about how things would work and how we will become the greatest code writer of all time.

You may feel that nothing will go wrong and that you will be able to manage everything in no time.

And one of the major fallacies that will arise with the job that we want to perform here is that we believe we don't need any sort of coding assistance at all. While it would be fantastic to begin coding in any language, including C#, without any assistance, we must face reality and remember that we will learn more quickly and efficiently when we have the correct type of peer feedback and mentors to assist us.

When someone with more expertise comes in and can help out, what may seem to be an impossible bug to deal with or a subject that appears to be unlearnable when you tackle it on your own, things become a lot simpler; and you may really learn something new. You should never be afraid to seek for assistance, whether online or in person. All of the more sophisticated programmers you see now were once in your shoes.

And most developers will be overjoyed that they will be able to code again, and will be more than glad to assist you with some of the codings that you want assistance with. Of course, we must be cautious and not take advantage of this at any point along the process.

The greatest guideline to follow here is to never ask someone to assist you figure out anything with your code for more than 20 minutes. And you should not seek for assistance until you have spent at least 20 minutes researching how it works and what you can do with it beforehand.

Take Rest Periods

There will be moments when you are writing out some of the C# code that you want to accomplish, and you will get stuck on something.

You work on it for a while, but it just seems to make things worse.

You keep trying and working at it, effectively exacerbating the issue or failing to locate it at all, and your irritation levels rise. You want to be able to repair the issue and go back to coding, but all you end up doing is becoming angry and the codes become more jumbled. When this occurs, and it is something that may happen to anybody, we must take a break. This is perhaps the last thing we want to think about while working with the C# language and some of our code, but it will enable us to take a break from the issue and get some fresh air, or at the very least do anything else for a while. And, frequently, when you take a break and then return to it, you will discover that the issue, which appeared insurmountable at first, is really rather simple to resolve.

No one likes to give up after putting in so much time and work, but in the long run, it may reduce frustration and guarantee that you can patch up your code in no time.

Make use of the C# Community

When it comes time to perform our coding in the C# language and more, one of the cool things we'll discover is that there is a big community of various programmers and developers along the route that can help you out.

These communities will comprise a large number of programmers who have participated in all phases of the process. Others are new to the game, some have been playing for a while, and some are more experienced. This is fantastic news for you since it gives us the opportunity to go through and learn a lot of stuff. We may ask folks who live in the neighborhood questions. We can locate many of the codes we need to work on a range of applications and learn something new. And we get to chat to other people about the programming language, meet new people, and ask a lot of questions along the road. It is a good idea for you to go through this process to ensure that you can really locate a community that works for you. There are a plethora of these communities available online, and we just need to choose the one that seems to be the greatest fit for us. This is a terrific location to go if you're having troubles with your codes or if you'd want to find out anything that isn't working out so well for your code to begin with.

Make use of the provided sample codes.

While this handbook takes the effort to offer you a few instances of codes to demonstrate how all of the various forms of coding are meant to operate, just looking through the code is not enough to enhance your comprehension.

To get a thorough understanding, spend some time running and tinkering with the code to discover what it can accomplish.

The more time you can devote to working on the code, the better off you will be in the long run.

The example codes that you will work with are packed in a way that the reader can easily understand with the inclusion of things like instructions and comments. However, you will discover that they are occasionally difficult to reproduce from scratch.

Reading is not the same as comprehending, and really going through the process of putting down part of the code on your own and then executing it will ensure that you can learn how to code much quicker than previously. The more time we can spend creating and practicing some of the codes we uncover, trying them out, and tinkering with them, the simpler the coding language will be along the road.

This is an excellent technique to ensure that we can understand what is going on, what will not work when we make adjustments, and much more in the process. Reading the code may work in certain circumstances, and it may seem to be the better alternative to work with, but it will not teach us the most efficient approach to construct your own applications.

Working with the C# programming language is an excellent option.

There are several possibilities available to us, and it is a viable solution for the majority of the applications that we want to develop. Even as someone who is totally new to the field of programming and has never done any coding before, I will find the C# language to be a fantastic choice to work with. When you are ready to begin the process of learning a new coding language, you will discover that following recommendations will help you get started on the right foot.

Thank you for reading through C# for Beginners; we hope it was educational and provided you with all of the skills you needed to reach your objectives, whatever they may be.

The next step is to get started with some of the many codes provided in this handbook and take your time learning more about how this language will work for your specific requirements.

If you've determined that the C# programming language is the one for you, you're in good company. Many programmers throughout the globe will use this language, and now that you've finished this manual, you may join them. There is so much knowledge and information in this handbook that we can use that you will find it to be one of the greatest alternatives that we have when it comes to working with the C# language. We looked at the classes and objects, how to write our code, how to deal with loops and conditional expressions, and so much more.

When all of this comes together and combines, you will discover that developing your programs is straightforward and quick, and you will be able to do it in no time. This handbook takes the time to teach us more about the C# programming language and what it can accomplish for us.

When you're ready to become a programming expert and make all of this code work for you, be sure to check out this handbook to get started. Finally, if you found this book beneficial in any way, please leave a review on Amazon!